Mallorca

Majority of photographs supplied by: COFIBA *distribuciones*, S.L.

Design, phototypesetting and printing: ingrama/sa (GRAFICAS GARCIA) Inca (Mallorca)

D.L. P.M. 839 - 1997
ISBN: 84-85932-22-6

DISTRIBUTION
EXCLUSIVE SALE

COFIBA
distribuciones, S.L.

C/. Aldea de Cariño, 16 A
Tel. 73 68 97 • Fax: 73 71 31
07011 PALMA DE MALLORCA

The Island of Mallorca

Mallorca is the largest of the Balearic Islands. It covers an area of 3,640 square kilometres and its scenery is very varied. From the mountains of the Serra de Tramuntana which sweep down to the sea as spectacular cliffs to the plains in the interior or the immense sandy beaches in the south. The result of this diversity is an island that offers the attractions of beach and mountain, entertainment and culture. And, in a typically sunny and mild Mediterranean climate.

Palma, the Mallorcan capital, sums up the international character of an island that has become the leading holiday resort in the Mediterranean.

$\mathcal{B}$Bay of Palma

The Cathedral (*La Seu*) is the most well known building in Palma. Construction began in the XIIIth. century on the site of a Mussulman mosque. It is considered to be the finest example of Mediterranean Gothic architecture in that the sensations of light and length are dominant features in comparison with the shadows and height of European Gothic buildings. The light passing through the large rose window made from 1,236 pieces of coloured glass is extremely impressive. The central nave has a height of 44 metres and its interior was renovated by the Catalan architect Antoni Gaudí at the beginning of this century.

Mallorca Cathedral seen from the fishermen's quay.

The rose window in La Seu dominates the three naves of the Gothic church.

Palma has an imposing sea facade. The *Palacio de Almudaina* is next to the Cathedral. The Romans founded the first Palma there in I B.C. Later it was the residence of the Mussulmen governors before becoming the court of the Kings of Mallorca in the XIIIth. and XIVth. centuries. Not far off, the *Sa Llonja* building (XVth. century), headquarters of the College of Merchants and one of the leading attractions of the city. At its side the old *Consulat de Mar* which now house the Offices of the President of the Balearic Autonomous Government.

Effects of the light on the interior of La Seu in Palma.

The Cathedral dominates the spacious public Parc de la Mar and is reflected in the waters beneath.

Palma Cathedral forms an architectural masterpiece with the stretch of Renaissance wall and the Palacio de la Almudaina (in the background).

Statue of Nuredduna, the legendary figure created by the poet Miquel Costa i Llobera, in the Passeig Marítim.

Gardens of Arabic influence in s'Hort del Rei at the foot of the Palacio de la Almudaina.

Sa Llonja, masterpiece of Gothic civil building, by the Mallorcan architect Guillem Sagrera.

The Passeig Marítim, the maritime showcase of the Mallorcan capital.

The presence of La Seu dominates the traditional fishermen's quay.

The Consulat de Mar, in the Passeig Sagrera is a building of Renaissance origin.

*The Cathedral and la Almudaina dominate
the maritime facade of Palma.*

The city of Palma stretches across the horizon of the Bay. In the background, the Playa de Palma holiday resort. In the foreground, the suburb of Génova.

Exterior of the Castillo de Bellver, a circular fortification constructed in the XIIIth. century.

Castillo de Bellver dominates the entire city and justifies its name- beautiful view.

Statue of Rey Jaume I in the
Plaça de España.

Palma is a hospitable and cosmopolitan city. Side by side with its tourist attractions such as the *Pueblo Español*, it preserves the buildings and monuments that speak of its history, Gothic and Baroque churches, convents and Modernist buildings like the old *Gran Hotel*, the first to open on the Island, and nowadays a cultural centre.

The Pueblo Español seen from the outside.

The Gran Hotel building is the best example of Modernism in Mallorca.

The gardens of La Alhambra in Granada reproduced in the Pueblo Español.

*The Pueblo Español in Palma combines reproductions
of the most important buildings in Spain.*

The Old Quarter of Palma has a great deal of character. Certain corners are still reminiscent of the Mussulman *Medina Mayurka*. That town was made up of narrow dark lanes which opened onto gardens and palaces. One of the most well-known buildings dating from that time is the *Arab Baths* in calle Serra, with its lovely cupola sustained by columns. In spite of the long Mussulman rule, there are few architectural remains of that time, in Mallorca.

Reproduction of the Arabic style in the Pueblo Español in Palma.

Interior of the Arab baths in calle Serra with the light entering through the domed roof of its cupola.

Plaza Juan Carlos I in the upper
region of the Passeig del Born.

Sant Francesc has the
loveliest Gothic
cloisters in Mallorca.

The aristocratic features of Palma date mainly from the XVIIth. and XVIIIth centuries when the noble families commissioned elegant mansions in the Italian style. Their courtyards, one of the most characteristic features of this period, have become a symbol of the city. As the streets were still very narrow the entrances were made to provide light and space, on the basis of columns, arcades and stairs of honour. The courtyards were, therefore, the outward show of the wealth and standing of the family. And they continue to be a leading attraction for visitors.

The city also has important chur-ches, generally Gothic to begin with but modified during the Baroque period as can be seen in *Sant Francesc* or *Santa Eulàlia* in the centre of the city. And, in the same area, certain convents like *Santa Clara* still preserve all their original features and look the same as they did centuries ago.

A stroll through old Palma enables you to discover a city existing apart from the hustle and bustle of visitors - mansions, churches and narrow lanes where the past is still present.

The courtyard of Ca'n Oleza in calle Morey, is one of the best known in Palma.

Courtyard of the Brotherhood of Sant Pere and Sant Bernat Building in the street of the same name.

*Can Pereantoni, a beach
next to Palma.*

The Bay of Palma is embra-
ced by extensive beaches. *Ca'n
Pereantoni Beach*, on the same
side as the *Parc de la Mar* and the
city, is next to the small harbour
of *Es Portixol* and the *Es Molinar*
Promenade. But the biggest
beach can be found in the area
between *Ca'n Pastilla* and
S'Arenal where the sands stretch
for five kilometres. It is the leading
holiday resort on the Island.

S'Arenal, the most famous beach on the Island.

The Playa de Palma with its long sandy beach and the city in the background.

The thatched sunshades are a characteristic feature of beaches like Ca'n Pastilla.

From Playa de Palma to S'Arenal, the Bay is one immense beach.

*Marina in
Ca'n Pastilla.*

The Bay of Palma is not
only beaches and hotels. Its
other attractions include
entertainment and leisure
activities with innumerable
restaurants, shops and discos, making this area almost
a second city during the
summer months.

Gardens in Playa de Palma.

As night falls, the Playa de Palma becomes an animated centre of entertainment and fun.

Arenal Beach lies in the Municipality of Llucmajor and is a continuation of Playa de Palma.

Palm trees and yachts form part of the image of S'Arenal.

Aerial view of Cala Major.

On the western side, the Bay of Palma also has beaches and holiday centres. Thus, from *Cala Major* to *Illetes*, in the Municipality of *Calvià* there is small beach after beach with hotels and apartments. Many Palma people choose to live there because of its proximity to the city. This is also the location of the *Palacio de Marivent*, summer home of the Royal Family.

Holiday makers riding through S'Arenal.

Illetes, with the small islet that gave it its name.

The area of *Illetes* received its name from the two islets along its coastline. As it is so close to Palma, it is one of the most popular places for city people to spend a day on the beach, in the midst of pine woods and overlooking the panoramic view of the Bay.

Cala Major coast with the Palacio de Marivent in the background.

*Portals
Vells
Beach.*

West Coast

*Old windmill at the entrance
to Santa Ponça.*

The west coast is the most tourist-orientated in Mallorca. The *Calvià* area includes such important centres as *Palmanova, Magalluf, Santa Ponça* and *Peguera*. There, the attractions of beach and countryside are combined with a wide range of leisure activities and services as befits one of the largest holiday municipalities in Spain. Continuing on, the *Andratx* area has some spectacular scenery and the busy harbour and marina of *Port d'Andratx*. Finally the islet of *Sa Dragonera* has been declared a Natural Park and is yet another of the exceptional features of the Island.

The old oratory in Portals Nous looks down over Puerto Portals Beach.

The Palmanova beaches have been remodelled with a modern promenade walk and all ancillary services.

Aerial view of Palmanova in the foreground with Magalluf in the background.

Magalluf Beach with the islet of Sa Porrassa in the background.

The holiday resort of *Magalluf*, one of the liveliest in Mallorca, came into being in the sixties, on land that had been marshes for centuries. It has a long beautiful sandy beach with innumerable bars, restaurants, discos and places of entertainment which have become the Mecca of youthful holiday makers of all nationalities. Opposite *Magalluf* is *Sa Porrassa* Islet with its characteristic outline.

*The holiday resort of Magalluf is one of
the liveliest in the area.*

*Magalluf Promenade,
next to the beach.*

*The Malgrat Isles from the mirador
above Santa Ponça.*

*Cala Vinyes, close to the
Mallorca Casino.*

Santa Ponça was a small port
even in the old days, in use in
Roman and medieval times. On
the peak of *Puig de sa Morisca*,
there are the remains of a
prehistoric settlement. Today it
is a hotel and residential centre
which is known for its extensive

*Panoramic view of Santa Ponça with
Puig de sa Morisca in the background.*

beach, bordered by stately pines.

    Peguera also has areas of great beauty. Apart from *Torà* and *dels Morts* beaches, there is the small *Cala Fornells*, with *Caló d'es Monjo*, which is very popular with divers given its considerable depth. Here is a combination of pine trees, transparent waters and cliffs with a leading Mediterranean holiday centre.

Santa Ponça Beach.

Aerial view of Peguera and its two beaches.

The Peguera Promenade with Cap Andritxol in the background.

Peguera beaches have all the most modern services.

Cala Fornells, one of the singular corners of Costa de Calvià.

A peaceful scene in Cala Fornells.

Camp de Mar Beach in the Municipality of Andratx.

At the far end of Port d'Andratx, the boats are a reminder of the fishing origins of the harbour.

Sant Elm with Pantaleu Islet in the foreground.

(Left). Imposing aerial view of La Mola Promontory with Port d'Andratx in the background.

𝒩orth Coast

*Marble mirador in Son Marroig,
built by Archduke Ludwig Salvator.*

The most spectacular views in Mallorca are to be found on the North coast. The mountains in the *Serra de Tramuntana* rise over a blue horizon, amid woods, and cliffs above deep blue waters. Scenes whose majesty and beauty are reflected in the works of many painters. The *Tramuntana* coastline is closely linked with the historical figure of the Archduke Ludwig Salvator, a member of the Austro-Hungarian Imperial Family who bought several properties in the area, conserving the countryside and building miradors to enjoy it.

The Ricardo Roca mirador is one of the best places for admiring the north coast of Estellencs.

The atalaya de Ses Animes in Banyalbufar, an old defence watchtower which looms over the precipice.

Estellencs is a stone coloured village which lies between the foothills of Mount Galatzó and the sea.

The northern Mallorcan coast still preserves the memory of past centuries when life was difficult because of pirate raids. The economy of these villages was based on fishing, livestock raising and some farming. *Banyalbufar* was famous for its wine and you can still see the spectacular system of stone terraces built to grow the vines. *Deià*, a small fishing village, became the home of writers and artists, particularly after Robert Graves, the British writer and poet and author of *I, Claudius*, made its name known throughout the world.

The Ses Animes defence tower brings to mind the pirate raids.

The terraces where the vines are grown are a feature of the Banyalbufar countryside.

Sa Foradada is a small peninsula recognisable from the hole which can be seen in its upper part. It used to be part of the Son Marroig property owned by the Archduke Ludwig Salvator.

Panoramic view of Deià on the sides of Teix Mountain.

Cala de Deià is one of the loveliest places on the northern coast and preserves all its Mediterranean character.

The harmony of the countryside of the small village of Llucalcari between Deià and Sóller has been a favourite choice of many painters.

One of the most famous places in Mallorca is the town of *Valldemossa*. It achieved literary recognition in the book *A Winter in Mallorca* written when Frederick Chopin and George Sand stayed in its *Cartuja*, or monastery, between 1838 and 1839. The cell where they stayed is visited by thousands of visitors in an atmosphere which has changed very little since then, in the midst of gardens, tranquillity and an attractive view. Nowadays, the cloisters of the *Cartuja* are used for musical festivals held in memory of Chopin.

Mementos of the stay of Chopin and George Sand in the Cartuja.

The buildings of the Cartuja in Valldemossa dominate the entire valley.

The Coll de Sóller Road which descends to the town through many bends.

The tourist train of Sóller travels through lovely scenery which conserves the character of earlier times.

The *Sóller* valley, located in the foothills of the highest mountains on the Island is a world of its own within Mallorca. Famous for its oranges, it was orientated to France for many years where it exported its agricultural products. Other villages in the valley are *Fornalutx* and *Biniaraix* whose stone buildings nestle in the green of olive and fruit trees, to the sound of torrents and lovely views of the mountains. Scenery which cannot be found in any other location in Mallorca.

The tourist train of Sóller travels through lovely scenery which conserves the character of earlier times.

Panoramic view of the Sóller Valley with the Serra de Tramuntana in the background.

The Sóller Train Station is in one of the Modernist buildings in the town.

*Port de
Sóller, now
a leading
holiday
resort, used
to be the
centre for
exporting
citrus fruit
to France.*

The small village of Fornalutx whose stone houses nestle among olive and fruit trees.

Biniaraix is located by a spectacular ravine which acts as the setting for a popular meeting of painters.

The Sa Calobra road is so narrow and winding that part of it is known to some as the "knot in a tie".

Further north, the Mallorcan coast becomes more barren and spectacular. The great mountains fall down to the seas in precipices and torrents and there are few ports or harbours. This is the setting for the area of *Sa Calobra* whose greatest attraction is the nearby *Torrent de Pareis*. An enormous pass in the rocks with scenery that seems to be from a lost world. The *Torrent de Pareis* is a favourite place for excursions and also acts as the backcloth to choir concerts as its acoustics are extraordinary. In the upper part of the range are the reservoirs of *Cuber* and *Gorg Blau*, and *Lluc Monastery*, the spiritual heart of the Island.

Sa Calobra Jetty at the mouth of the Torrent de Pareis.

Sa Calobra Beach surrounded by high mountains.

Mouth of the Torrent de Pareis, a narrow pass gouged out of the rocks.

*The Torrent de Pareis reaches the sea at a small sandy beach
which is one of the most well-known beauty spots in Mallorca.*

Aerial view of the reservoirs of Cuber and Gorg Blau on the "roof" of Mallorca.

Lluc Monastery is the place most venerated by Mallorcans. Every summer there is a walk on foot from Palma to Lluc.

Pollença is a town of interesting old buildings particularly when seen from the Calvary steps.

Pollença has an ancient Roman bridge.

Cala de Sant Vicenç with the impressive wall of Cavall Bernat in the background.

Aerial view of Port de Pollença in the Bay closed by the Formentor Promontory to the north.

*The beaches in Port de Pollença domin-
ate the bay of the same name closed by
Cabo Formentor to the north and Cabo
Pinar to the south.*

Cabo Formentor is the extre-
me north of Mallorca. It has scenes of grandeur and desolation,
high barren mountains and an
endless horizon. Close by, *Port
de Pollença* has changed from a
small fishing village to a leading
holiday centre

*The Port de Pollença promenade is still lined
by small family houses, side by side with
modern hotels and apartments.*

Panoramic view of Formentor with the Hotel of the same name.

Formentor Promontory is another famous beauty spot in Mallorca, particularly from the mirador overlooking Es Colomer Isle.

View of the Formentor Peninsula with the Isles of Es Colomer (left) and Formentor (right). At the end of the promontory is a lighthouse which faces Minorca.

M a l l o r c a

*Mal Pas
Beach
among
pines with
Pollença
and
Formentor
Mountains
silhouetted
in the back-
ground.*

𝒩 ortheast Coast

*The medieval
walls of
Alcúdia are
a reminder
of its historic
past when it
was a strong
town that
guarded the
Bay.*

The northeastern coast of Mallorca extends from *the Bahía de Alcúdia* to the coves in the *Artà* area. It is open countryside which combines holiday centres with cultural attractions such as the ruins of the Roman city of *Pollentia* (in Alcúdia) and the *s'Albufera* Natural Park. Some beaches are wide, with fine white sand, but there are also rocky beaches of great beauty and small coves.

Alcúdia is a town of great historical interest. Here was the site of the Roman town of Pollentia, the most important of its day. And the Renaissance walls are still well preserved.

S'Illot, on the Alcúdia coast, looks out to Formentor.

Panoramic view of the Aucanada coast, one of the loveliest places in Alcúdia.

The pine woods in Aucanada reflected in the waters of the sea.

Interior of the Ermita de la Victòria at the foot of the mountain of the same name.

The beaches of Port d'Alcúdia are immense stretches of sand.

Alcúdia Bay consists of old dunes and pinewoods, nowadays the setting of the leading holiday centres, *Port d'Alcúdia, Playa de Muro* and *Ca'n Picafort,* which border the sea, overlooking a bay, closed by the Victoria Mountains on the one side and *Cap Ferrutx* on the other. The countryside is being conserved in such areas as the *s'Albufera* and in the coastal fringe of *Sa Canova.*

In the area close to s'Albufera,
holiday homes and hotels line the
canals which gives them
a special personality.

*Night view of the Port d'Alcúdia promenade, one of
the liveliest tourist centres in the Bay.*

*Palm trees and thatched
sunshades bordering
the Alcúdia beaches.*

Ca'n Picafort grew from a
small group of summer houses
into one of the leading tourist
centres in the area. Its extensive
beach, situated in the centre of
the Alcúdia Bay, is long and
lovely.

*The dunes reach right down to the sea giving the Alcúdia
Bay its characteristic aspect.*

Several torrents empty into Alcúdia Bay forming small wetland areas of great charm.

Ca'n Picafort, in the Municipality of Santa Margalida, is a well-known holiday centre.

Ca'n Picafort is bounded to the east by the Son Bauló Torrent which can be seen in the right of the photograph.

Son Bauló Beach, next to the torrent, with the silhouette of Cabo Ferrutx in the background.

The coast of Colònia de Sant Pere in the Municipality of Artà is rocky and wild with a special attraction.

The town of Capdepera was protected by its walls during the time of the pirate raids.

Capdepera is the most easterly point in Mallorca.

Cala Mesquida, with its extensive white sand, is one of the loveliest beaches in the Capdepera area.

Cala Guya, close to Cala Ratjada, looking towards its neighbouring island of Minorca.

Cala Lliteres is another holiday resort on the north-eastern coast of Mallorca.

The Cala Ratjada Lighthouse looms over Mallorca's eastern sea.

A corner of Cala Gat surrounded by pines and the typical "palmitos" or small palm trees of the area.

Cala Ratjada is another example of a small fishing centre that, over time, has become a tourist resort of importance. It has preserved its early beginnings with its small harbour and traditional summer homes. This is the closest point of Mallorca to Minorca which is on the other side of the channel and can be seen to the northwest on clear days.

Son Moll Beach, typical scenery of the northeasterly coast of Mallorca.

Cala Ratjada, a lively and attractive fishing port and harbour.

Panoramic view of Cala Ratjada (left), Capdepera Lighthouse and Cala Guya to the right.

E ast Coast

*Tourist train
in Cala
Millor.*

The eastern or *Llevant* coast consists of numerous coves where tourist resorts have sprung into being since the sixties and seventies. From *Canyamel* to *Cala Santanyí*, quiet countryside with pines and sandy beaches unfolds in this area of Mallorca. There are no big resorts or towns and the summer atmosphere is a peaceful family one. Here are the famous caves of *Artà* and *Drac*, among the leading tourist attractions in Mallorca. Boat trips along the coast or across to the nearby *Cabrera* Land-Sea National Park can be arranged in any of the coves.

Panoramic view of Canyamel Beach, a base for visiting Artà Caves.

Cala Bona is an old fishing port which still preserves its original character.

Cala Millor, in the Municipality of Son Servera, is one of the leading holiday centres in the area. The urbanisation grew up around a spacious sandy beach during the sixties. It is a wide open space without an excessive amount of buildings and has, on the north, the mountain foothills of the Artà area.

The extensive sandy beach is one of the main attractions of Cala Millor.

Cala Millor which came into being with the tourist boom of the sixties.

*Visitors to
Cala Millor,
mainly
German in
the
beginning,
continue to
look for a
quiet family
atmosphere.*

Sa Coma beach with the pine woods of Punta de n'Amer in the background.

Sa Coma lies to the side of the promontory of *Punta de n'Amer*, a protected natural area, and which is characterised most of all by its defence tower, dating from the XVIIth. century, which dominates the area. It is a holiday resort which originated in the seventies, comprising mainly family houses. Its sandy beach is really outstanding, with panoramic views over the *Llevant* coast.

S'Illot spreads across both sides of the torrent which opens on the beach.

S'Illot is another tourist centre which has developed over the
last few decades. It surrounds the
mouth of a torrent with a rocky
spur which makes up the small
islet that gave it its name. There
was a prehistoric settlement here
and its walls and dwellings are
still preserved in what is, nowadays, a landscaped area.

Portocristo is the holiday centre of the Manacor area where the famous caves of Drac and Hams are to be found.

Cala Anguila, close to Portocristo, shows the typical coastal formation from the courses of two torrents on their journey to the sea.

Cala Romántica in the Municipality of Manacor with its rocky spur and sandy beach.

Calas de Mallorca one of the leading beach resorts on the Manacor coast.

The vivid blues and greens of the water on the east coast can be seen in small coves and caves formed by erosion.

Cala Tropicana is another of the typical east coast beaches.

View of Cala Murada in the Municipality of Manacor.

Portocolom is a spectacular inlet on the Felanitx coast used for centuries as a fishing port and is, nowadays, a tourist and residential area.

Cala Marçal in the south of Portocolom is one of the most frequented beaches on the Island.

Cala Serena where the pine woods reach almost to the edge of the sea.

Cala Sa Nau is a narrow beach, located at the mouth of an ancient torrent.

The most southerly area on this coast enters the Municipality of *Santanyí*. The landscape changes colour, with more ochre shades and, inland, it is much flatter. The tourist resorts have their own special character, with the houses spilling down to the small harbours. Here is the *Cala Mondragó*, a lovely natural area with an extraordinary range of greens and blues.

Aerial view of the Cala Llonga area.

Cala Llonga harbour, close to Cala d'Or has a great deal of personality.

Small coves such as Es Fortí are a characteristic feature of this area in the south of Mallorca.

Cala d'Or is the most important holiday centre on the Santanyí coast.

Cala Egos, close to Portopetro still preserves all the charm of the eastern coast.

The small harbour at Portopetro still preserves its seafaring air in spite of modern tourism.

Caló d'en Burgit can be found between Cala de sa Barca Trencada and Cala Mondragó.

Spectacular panoramic view of the protected area of Cala Montdragó.

Cala Figuera stretches along a narrow inlet on the coast.

Cala Santanyí amid pine woods and small cliffs.

South Coast

The harbour of Colònia Sant Jordi, close to Cabo Salinas which is the most southerly point of the Island.

The south coast of Mallorca has its own special features. Surrounded by flat gently coloured countryside, it has wide and spectacular beaches such as the sandy *Es Trenc* beach as well as narrow coves such as *Cala Pi*. The archipelago of *Cabrera* can be seen on the horizon. It is a Land-Sea National Park. Here you can still see the old salt flats and inland you can visit important archeological sites such as *Capocorb Vell*.

Colònia
Sant Jordi
lies between
large
beaches: Es
Trenc on the
one side and
Es Dolç and
Es Carbó on
the other.

The landscape of Es Trenc features a scrubland plain, ancient dunes, very white sand and water in very shade of green.

The *Cabrera Archipelago* has been a Land-Sea National Park since 1991. In addition, to the large island or *Cabrera Gran*, it also includes six islets. It is an almost unspoilt area and therefore enables you to discover what the Mediterranean landscape was like before the advent of tourism.

It is of great ecological and historical importance and it can be visited on organised excursions from *Colònia de Sant Jordi*. In the port, there is a castle from the XIVth. century and one of its most curious features is *Cova Blava* where the water is an almost unbelievable range of blues.

Cala Pi is a beach formed by an ancient torrent, surrounded by woods and in a landscape of great beauty.

Aerial view of Cabrera Gran. At right and in the foreground, the Punta Enciola Lighthouse. Further north, the harbour. And, in the background, the islet of Conillera.

The landscape of Cabrera remains untouched by the passage of the years.

Rural Regions

The windmills on the Pla are a familiar feature of Mallorca.

The most well-known image of Mallorca is its coastline. Nevertheless, for centuries life on the Island went on inland. The beaches and cliffs were unproductive places and dangerously exposed to pirate raids. Therefore in order to discover the real heartbeat of Island life you have to visit its rural regions - *el Raiguer,* which stretches along the foot of the *Serra de Tramuntana, el Pla* in the heart of the Island or *el Migjorn,* the most southerly area. Life has changed little in these areas which are far away from tourism.

The centre of rural life in Mallorca was the *possessió*, a cluster of houses in the country which apart from the manor house included those of the workers who took part in the agricultural work or looked after the livestock. Some of these *Possessiós* reached considerable size as can be seen in *Es Calderers de Sant Joan* or *Sa Granja de Esporles* both of which can be visited. These places maintain a way of life which is still followed today.

The village of Estellencs has survived for centuries on a mountain economy.

The kitchen and the large fireplace were the centre of life in the Mallorcan "Possessiós", or country manors.

The courtyards and the entrances to some of the "Possessiós" have a very aristocratic appearance at times.

The rural way of early times is reproduced in some "Possessiós" such as Sa Granja in Esporles.

View of the belltower in Inca, a town in the centre of the Island engaged in leatherwork.

The old water wheels, a legacy of the Arabs, are a witness of earlier times.

One of the most typical sights of the Mallorcan countryside - the almond blossom which fills the winter fields with its delicate colours.

*The villages of el
Raiguer, such as
Campanet, are
located in the
foothills of the
northern range of
mountains.*

*Many
"Possessiós" are
isolated in the
countryside
and are small
worlds of
selfsufficiency*

Manacor Church was renovated in the XIXth. century in the Neo-Gothic style.

The old inn at Alaró Castle.

The historical wealth of the old buildings in Mallorca is very important. In addition to the archeological treasures of *Pollentia* and *Capocorb Vell*, there are medieval castles on the Island that dominate their surroundings from their strategic heights, such as *Alaró*, *Santueri* or the *Castell de Rei*. Village parish churches are always interesting. Sometimes they have the look of a cathedral as can be seen in *Sineu*. And, finally, the hermitages and sanctuaries, all over the Island, are well worth a visit.

A forest of stalactites in the Cuevas dels Hams.

The nature of the ground in Mallorca favours the formation of great caves where, for centuries, water has carved strange forests of stalactites and stalagmites. There are four well-known groups of caves on the Island. Those at *Artà,* in the *Municipality of Capdepera,* are enormous and most impressive. In *Manacor* there are the *Cuevas dels Hams* and the *Cuevas del Drac,* with its famous underground lake. And in *Campanet* there are others, smaller in size, but very interesting.

The lake in the Cuevas del Drac is a well-known feature of Mallorca.

Orient, in a tiny mountain valley, is one of the smallest hamlets in Mallorca. Its houses and streets retain the tranquillity and atmosphere of other times.

Handcrafted glass is another well-known feature of Mallorca and dates from the XIVth. century. The Gordiola Company continues to use the traditional methods.

The evocative and romantic Alfàbia Gardens in Bunyola.

Spinning wool was one of the typical tasks in the "Possessiós" or manor farms and continues still at Sa Granja in Esporles

Sa Granja is an example of what the great rural Mallorcan mansions were like for centuries.

The material known as "llengos" or tongues is typical of the Island and is a very traditional element in furnishing Mallorcan homes, today.

There is a wide range of traditional pastries and cakes in Mallorca. Its "ensaimada" is renowned throughout the world.

Hand-made candles in Sa Granja in Esporles.

Vilafranca de Bonany with its fruit and vegetable shops lining the main street.

Inland markets are still held all over Mallorca. The one at Sineu is well-known throughout the Island.

Pottery is one of the leading skilled crafts in Mallorca and the most important potteries are in Pòrtol and Sa Cabaneta.

*The "siurell" is a small figure painted in white with a whistle in one side.
It is very old, dating from Arab times and, according to legend, it brings good fortune
if blown three times on the night of the full moon.*